W9-CRV-717

LISTENING WITH THE HEART

and Other Communication Skills

LISTENING WITH THE HEART

and Other Communication Skills

Sara Bhakti, Ph.D.

Published by Gaea Center
for Healing and Serving the Earth

Published by:
Gaea Center
for Healing and Serving the Earth
P.O. Box 652
Santa Cruz, CA 95061
USA

Library of Congress Catalog Card Number 91 – 73911
ISBN 0 – 9630514 – 0 – 7

Text set in 11 pt. Palatino
Printed on recycled paper

About the cover: Artist Lynne Feldman created this drawing especially for *LISTENING WITH THE HEART*. She is a painter and illustrator who is becoming known for her work celebrating family gatherings. She lives with her husband and two children in Rochester, New York.

ACKNOWLEDGMENTS

I wish to express my appreciation to my mother for her many years of listening to me with her heart; to my sister Fay for the generous gifts of her time, interest, editing skills, and Strunk; to my sister Barbara for reminding me to take down the scaffolding; and to my friends Pat and Bill Cane of IF for their enthusiastic assistance and guidance through the production process. Kudos to artist Lynne Feldman for creating a meaningful cover.

Especially, I wish to thank my clients, with whom and for whom the ideas expressed here have become more clear.

Contents

Introduction

Relationships are rather like dancing. We teach each other our rhythms and take turns leading and following. Learning to dance together, we try not to step on each other's toes. The purpose of communication skills is to facilitate the flow of our interactions with others so that we can harmonize our rhythms and enjoy being together as much of the time as possible.

If a person who likes tennis and wants to play even better consults a tennis pro, the pro will observe the player on the court, scrutinize the strokes, and recommend some changes, saying for example, "Remember to keep your wrist firm on the backhand." A single modification greatly improves the game.

So, too, with relationships. A few simple techniques improve our skill. With practice we will feel more confident giving information to, receiving from, and participating with others, whether in formal or casual sharing or in our most intimate relationships.

One of the things that make communication and relationships tricky is boundaries. With humans, many boundaries are ambiguous and changing. Only our physical bodies have distinct, fixed limits. Our mental, emotional, and spiritual selves are invisible and intangible. Communication skills respect these amorphous bodies, too. More about the physical, mental, emotional, and spiritual aspects of ourselves is found in the Afterword.

Another cause of failed communication, and hence failed relationships, is our disregard that other people are separate and equal, even children. Although as parents, guardians, or teachers we make decisions for and impose

2

requirements on children, their thoughts and feelings are entitled to the same respect as those of anyone else. By our ages, sizes, talents, and capabilities we are very dissimilar, but in relationships I recommend practicing the attitude that we are separate and equal. Successful communication and successful relationships depend not only on techniques to be acquired but also on attitudes to be learned and lived.

In the following pages, some components of good communication are set forth, simple techniques to improve your interactions with others. Three basic skills are presented: "I" messages, the "space between," and mirroring. These tools can help you not only to express what you want to say but also to listen effectively in order to create a harmonious, cooperative relationship with another person or group of people. The process of negotiation and methods for dealing with failed communication are described in the sections on negotiation and rage reduction. Finally, we pass beyond techniques and enter the area where communication becomes art, listening with the heart. Further applications of communication skills are briefly considered in the Afterword, and reference is given to a few books that are especially helpful.

1 "I" Messages

An "I" message is a statement that conveys information about the person speaking. Examples are sentences that begin with "I think...," "I feel...," "I wonder...," and "I need to know...." An "I" message is skillful primarily because it respects boundaries. Telling you about myself is the least threatening to you. An "I" message does not charge into or trample on the other person. It conveys information considerately without invasion. As with nations, so also with people: Boundaries are important.

BOUNDARIES

The boundaries of our physical bodies are obvious. We can see—and so can everyone else—where our bodies end at the surface of the skin. Our skin-encased bodies give us immediate feedback about our physical boundaries. If you were to bump into a wall, you would feel it. If you were to bump into another person, both of you would feel it. Furthermore, both sender and receiver can generally tell whether the touch was a soft caress or a shove. There are times when this is ambiguous, when the touch one person intended to send was received differently by the other. So even with the self-evident boundaries of our physical bodies, communication mix-ups may occur.

The boundaries of our emotional and mental bodies are not so well defined. Intangible and invisible, these boundaries are also changeable. Our emotional limits keep shifting, depending on our feelings at the time and on our relationship with the other person.

Consider the emotional boundaries between two lovers. At times there is a complete relaxing of the borders between them, a merging, which is one of the aspects that makes love-making so pleasurable: We have temporarily overcome our feeling of separation. This also accounts for why lovers' quarrels are so fraught with feeling. In a state of discord with our beloved, we feel separated. Our loved one does not feel the way we feel or think the way we think about a certain issue. We experience this as pain, an insulting reminder of our separateness. There—right in the relationship we chose to overcome it—we are faced again with the essential existential fact: our aloneness.

In communications it is skillful to consider emotional boundaries—your own and those of the person with whom you are talking. We know at some level when we are being invaded. Our feelings give us feedback.

THE PRONOUN "YOU" AND WHY TO AVOID IT

The pronoun "you" is intrusive. It penetrates into the emotional space of the other person. An example may

7

make this more clear. If someone wags a finger at us and begins to criticize our behavior, targeting something we have—or have not—done, we become defensive. Our stomachs may tighten up protectively as we ward off the verbal attack. We may even become so preoccupied with what we are going to say in our self-defense that we stop listening. As a communication method, this is not very satisfactory.

Observe yourself in conversation. Do you unwittingly violate the other person's mental or emotional boundaries with your words? Notice your use of the pronoun "you." Beware of telling others about themselves: what they are thinking, or feeling, or should be—or not be—doing. All of these are intrusions, invasions of their separate and equal space.

So rather than tell you about you, I will be a much more effective communicator by telling you about me. If it is in regard to something you have said or done, I will refer to your expression or action briefly and tell you its effect on me. For example, "When you said that," or "When you did that," or "When you weren't there," "I felt...," "I thought...," "I wondered...," "I needed to know...." When I express myself to you in this way, you are left clear of attack, your emotional boundaries are not violated, and there is a greater possibility that you will listen receptively to the information I am sending. Since a purpose of communication is to convey information, this is skillful.

Sometimes someone will demur, "That seems selfish, to be telling about myself." But selfish means concerned excessively with oneself; seeking one's own advantage or well-being without regard for others. In an "I" message, we are simply communicating information about ourselves to another person.

BEGINNING TO PRACTICE

Take a friend or relative into your confidence and explain that you want to practice "I" messages. Deliberately incorporate into your conversation with this person sentences that begin with "I think..."—followed by the expression of an idea, and "I feel..."—followed by the expression of an emotion or a physical sensation. Surprisingly often, people confuse "I think" with "I feel." Pay attention to which word you are using and follow through with the expression that matches.

Physical sensations are always involved in emotions.

Indeed, we cannot have feelings without them. A little self-scrutiny will reveal that this is so. The English language is rich with examples of sensations that connote emotions: "a lump in my throat," "butterflies in my stomach," "that gives me goose flesh," "hopping mad."

If you are having trouble with "I feel," a simple exercise may help. After reading these instructions, become comfortable and close your eyes. Focus your awareness on your feet. Just notice any sensations there. You may become aware of your feet feeling cold or warm, or of pressure where they are in contact with your shoes or with the floor or the bed. Simply register whatever physical sensation you become aware of and move on. Turn your attention next to the lower legs, then to the knees, the thighs, the buttocks, the abdomen, and the entire lower torso. Continue slowly, in a relaxed way, to move your awareness through the various parts of your body and simply note whatever sensations are there.

At the end of the exploration inside, ask yourself what you feel. Perhaps relaxed, perhaps tense; you may have become aware of tightness in certain parts of your body. Begin to notice yourself more. Incorporate into your daily experience awareness of your sensations and emotions.   Practice deliberately, telling yourself—or another person—at least once each day, "I feel...."

Here are some emotions that are commonly experienced by most people: joy, sadness, anger, happiness, worry, depression, excitement, fear, peace. Close your eyes and recall some emotions you have felt today. Note that the feelings or emotions we have are universal. Most human beings experience them to some degree. The stories that go with the feelings are our own unique personal histories.

You can turn the information your feelings give you into good communication skills by reporting them. For example, when you feel stuck for what to say, you can say *that*: "I'm feeling stuck for what to say." Or, "I'm feeling badgered," "I'm feeling too upset to listen," "I need more time to think about this," "I'm feeling angry... confused... sad... sick... my stomach's turning over...." When you grow accustomed to reporting your feelings, you keep current and your communications will have an in-the-moment quality of aliveness.

An "I" message gives one the opportunity to express thoughts and feelings, according to the discretion of the individual. It is skillful to know, given the situation or the other person(s) involved, just what or how much is appropriate to tell. To know what *not* to say is also skillful! Timing, knowing *when* to say, is also a skill.

The primary benefit of "I" messages is its respect for boundaries. Remembering to use "I" messages can greatly improve your ability to relate to others.

The second basic communication skill is the "space between," an unspoken attitude that also recognizes and respects boundaries.

2 The "Space Between"

I imagine the "space between" to be a circular space created whenever two or more people are communicating. The circle between them begins to fill up like a soup pot, accumulating not only the chunky bits of information but also the feeling or flavor each person puts in. After a time, a quality emerges that imparts the essence of their interchange; they can pause and regard it. Each encounter opens a new circle between them, a fresh beginning.

The one who is talking can be persuasive, eloquent, and impassioned about his or her point of view. By using "I" messages and delivering opinions into the "space between," the speaker demonstrates respect for the boundaries of the other person and conveys the attitude that this exchange is a giving of information, not a tug-of-war. The other person consequently will feel much safer and not assaulted when the sender communicates from this stance.

TUG-OF-WAR

Often communication appears to be a tug-of-war between two people, one trying to persuade—or drag—the other over to his or her point of view. In much communication the underlying message is, "Don't think the way you think, think the way I want you to think." Or, "Don't feel the way you feel, feel the way I want you to feel." This boils down to, "Think like I do," or "Feel like I do." In essence, "Don't be you—be me!" Once the absurdity of this unspoken attitude is recognized, it will be easier to stop yanking the other person with words. Preferably one will step back, stay within one's own borders, and give the information into the "space between." This is not only respectful but also effective. There is a greater chance that the information will be listened to.

Much as we may wish to control another person's thoughts and feelings, we have no right to. It may strike us as very inconvenient at times, but the other individual is always separate and equal, with his or her own point of view.

The "space between" offers protection just as "I" messages do. An "I" message respects boundaries by not invading the other person with finger-pointing accusations: "You this" and "You that." The "space between" respects boundaries by conveying the attitude that this is not a tug-of-war; one person is not trying to get the other to "Be me!"

GROUP WISDOM

There is another advantage to communicating into the "space between." The circle holds the shared wisdom of the group. When we pause to notice, the next appropriate expression or action often reveals itself.

I experienced a striking example of this as a silent observer at an international community over a period of day-long meetings. During this time the community was to decide an issue of major import: whether or not to buy the land on which they lived.

The physical arrangement of the meeting symbolized the process itself. The community was too large for its members to sit in a full circle. But the circle was represented symbolically by having some members sit in a curved row, facing the rest of the community who sat in tiers of curved rows. The front rows joined, forming a circular "space between."

The meeting was begun in prayerful silence. From time to time this silence was returned to, for purposes of refocusing or recentering the group. As in a Quaker meeting, members rose and spoke as each felt called to. Some spoke of their doubts, others spoke with conviction. Sometimes their words were impassioned, but always received in the silence. It actually began to feel as though a vast vessel was filling with the various, often contradictory points of view. All expressions were received into the "space between," the circle created by the front row of chairs.

It takes some maturity to release from one's position;

having delivered the information to not cling possessively to it, insistently lobbying for "my" way. Yet that is what I witnessed during this time.

The meeting was also a process, that is, learning was taking place as members informed one another and responded with new insights and considerations arising from what had already been said.

At the end of the time allotted for the process, a summary was made, a distillation of the group wisdom that had emerged. As an example of grass roots politics, the town-hall meeting of the future, it was inspiring and left a lasting impression on me. The focus of the group seemed centered on the situation, not losing sight of the commonly held desired outcome: that above all else, the decision be in the best interests of the community as a whole (substitute your "family," "household," "partnership"). When our awareness embraces our common ground, it becomes easier to surrender the possessive attachment to "my" particular point of view and the insistence that it prevail.

Thus the "space between" can be imagined as a circle between us that we fill with the content and feelings of our communication. It conveys an attitude that is respectful of boundaries.

Next, the technique of mirroring will be described, a form of active listening by which one person acknowledges what the other one has said.

3 Mirroring

Mirroring, as the word implies, is a reflecting back of what has just been said. Mirroring is the tool least used in conversations, but like an unmined crystal buried in the earth, its potential value awaits discovery.

In working with couples, I have partners mirror exactly, word for word. It is very revealing to each. Often one of the first things seen is how little of one partner's message is accurately taken in by the other. Mirroring back, most people cannot recall what was just said to them. Not very skillful communication! One of the factors quickly isolated is that people tend to send too much. The receiver is overwhelmed.

Mirroring reveals that if the partner is to fully receive, the sender needs to be more concise, to deliver sentences rather than paragraphs. In my practice, we often send the information phrase by phrase; sender and receiver quickly "tune in" to each other when both are concentrating.

Mirroring first of all ensures that you and your partner are working with the same information. It helps prevent the misunderstandings that come from not being heard accurately. Your partner and you both know whether the information sent has been correctly received.

In addition, mirroring gives the sender a chance to modify the message. Having heard the words repeated back, one can amend them: "I'm not a little angry; I'm furious!"

The biggest benefit from mirroring, the hidden gem discovered, is validation, the feeling we yearn for that "At last! Someone has heard me, someone understands."

Mirroring the other person's information is not the same thing as agreeing with it. Validation and agreement have been erroneously equated, especially in child rearing. For example, I ask seven-year-old Emily what she would like after the game. She replies, "Four hot dogs, a large coke, and a banana split!" Mirroring, I repeat back, "You want four hot dogs, a large coke, and a banana split!" "Yeah—make that five!" Both she and I know there is no way I am going to indulge her eyes at such expense to her stomach. But I can stay friendly, affectionate, acknowledging "Wow! You sound really hungry." Or, "That would be like New Year's, the Fourth of July, and your birthday all at once. Do you really think I'm going to let you eat all of that?" In short, we can always accept the other person's expression of feelings whether or not we agree with them.

Another important advantage of mirroring is, it slows things down. This has an effect similar to counting to ten, especially when feelings begin to escalate in an argument. Mirroring introduces a slower, more deliberate pace.

MIRRORING EXERCISE

Find someone with whom to practice. Choose a topic that has some emotional juice for you both. Then, facing each other, begin. Have your partner give a clear, brief "I" message into the space between you. Now mirror back to your partner, repeating word for word exactly what was said. Have your partner continue with the next "I" message into the "space between." Mirror that back, word for word. For example, Martha says to her friend: "I'm feeling sad." Her friend mirrors back, "You're feeling sad." Martha continues, "Yes, it's because you didn't walk home with me." Her friend mirrors, "It's because I didn't walk home with you." Martha: "And I'm worried that you don't like me anymore." Friend: "You're worried that I don't like you anymore." Martha: "I'm not even sure why—I don't know what happened." Friend: "You're not even sure why—you don't know what happened."

After your partner feels satisfied that the essence of the basic information has been expressed, change roles. Now it is your turn to *respond* to what your partner has said. Using "I" messages, add your information into the space between you. Have your partner mirror you, word for word.

Continuing our example, the friend might reply, "Well, I'm feeling angry." Martha mirrors, "You're feeling angry." Friend: "I waited for you for half an hour." Martha: "You waited for me for half an hour." Friend: "And when you weren't at the corner where I was expecting you, I got mad and left." Martha: "When I wasn't at the corner where you were expecting me, you got mad and left."

At the end of an agreed-upon time, perhaps fifteen minutes, stop. Briefly summarize the information that has been exchanged. In this example Martha would say, "I'm sad that you didn't walk home with me and worried about whether you still like me and wondering what happened. You're feeling angry because you waited half an hour, and when I wasn't there you got mad and left."

Now tell your partner what it was like for you to be mirrored. And listen, in turn, to what your partner experienced. Usually the person being mirrored appreciates the attention and feels grateful that his or her expressions have been received and validated. Notice that the focus is on the information being exchanged, and not on blaming or attacking one another. In this example, a few more rounds of "I" messages into the "space between" and mirroring will clarify the source of the misunderstanding: It seems that Martha had an expectation of a meeting time or place that her friend did not share.

When we develop skill at mirroring—but not until then—we can summarize the essence of what has been said, rather than repeating each sentence word for word. And we can bring out any unspoken feelings or emotions couched in the communication, making them explicit. For instance, if your son comes home from school looking dejected and sad, slumps down in a chair and stares listlessly at the floor, he has shown you how he is feeling before saying a word. As he tells you what is getting him down, in addition to mirroring the general sense of all he has said, you can also acknowledge the non-verbal expression of feeling that his body is modeling, saying kindly to him, "You look really down about that," or, "You seem pretty discouraged... sad... blue...." Show your respect for his boundaries by checking out your insight, asking him, "... are you?" This may help him learn to identify his feelings if he lacks a facility in expressing them directly.

Be careful not to tell others what they think or feel. You would have to be inside them to really know that! Show your respect for the boundaries of their mental and emotional bodies by checking out your assumptions. "You sound so excited..., are you?" "You look like you're about to cry, are you feeling sad about something?" "You seem irritated... frustrated... upset..., are you?"

In short, mirroring is a technique of reflecting back both the content and the feeling of what was just said, sentence by sentence. It lets us know that we heard accurately, it gives a feeling of validation (which is not the same thing as agreement), and it slows things down in an argument.

The three basic communication skills have now been presented: "I" messages; into the "space between"; and mirroring the information, the content as well as the feeling communicated. As you practice these methods, notice how they change and improve your interactions with others and whether you begin to feel more confident in talking over situations that arise.

The following sections treat some additional components of good communication: negotiation, and dealing with rage or out-of-control anger.

4 Negotiation

The steps of negotiation are the same as the initial communication skills: "I" messages, into the "space between," and mirroring. The spirit of negotiation is one of cooperation. The challenge is to look together for the flexibility, the tolerances, the places where there is some give to the situation.

Let us imagine a conversation between two people, Al and Bea. Al has sent a clear "I" message to Bea, into the space between them. Bea has mirrored, thereby indicating to Al that the message has been accurately received, and validating Al. Bea has, in turn, delivered an "I" message into the "space between" and been mirrored. After a few rounds of this, Al and Bea can acknowledge that the space between them contains all of the pertinent information that each has to say.

Now it is time to step back and assess the ingredients in the circle—the content or chunks of information and the feeling or flavor of the matter.

For example, suppose that Al has come home ravenously hungry and enthusiastic with plans to go out with Bea for pizza. Only to be told, "Oh, today I'm on an apple juice fast." "You're on an apple juice fast." "Umhmm."

Right here Al and Bea are at a choice point. In his disappointment, Al could begin to attack Bea, saying she's already entirely too thin, there is not much nutritional value in apple juice, etc. Bea, feeling defensive, could attack back, telling Al all the bad things about pizza: It's too greasy for his complexion, not a balanced meal, etc. Or they could get into a tug-of-war, each trying to persuade the other to change his or her mind: "Don't want what you want, want what I want you to want," which is a variation of "Don't be you—be me!"

With real skill, Al and Bea can choose an alternative: negotiation. "Well, if you're on an apple juice fast, shall I order in a small pizza and at least we can eat together?" "You want to order in pizza? But I'll feel too deprived to just be drinking apple juice. How about having your pizza out— and then we'll meet for a walk together... go to a movie together... read aloud to each other...."

There may be times when no negotiation is available. At those times, we can still acknowledge our disappointment: "That's lousy. You've come in full of enthusiasm for pizza. And here I am on my apple juice fast. It's pretty disappointing." "It sure is."

In negotiation, there are two basic steps: negotiation with one's self and negotiation with the other. The first person to negotiate with is yourself. Ask yourself, in an inner dialogue, "What do I want? What do I need?" And consider what your own boundaries are in this particular situation. Using the valuable information that your feelings give you, assess with your mind, "Given this situation," or, "Given this other person, what do I choose to say or to do?" Find the places where you can agree with yourself to be flexible, to modify your request. And brain-storm with yourself for alternative approaches—this is the creative, zesty part of problem solving. Especially helpful in negotiation with ourselves is the work of Ken Keyes on "upgrading addictive desires to preferences," in his fine book, *Handbook to Higher Consciousness* (see Suggested Reading).

Having negotiated with yourself, knowing how much you can give way and where your tolerances are, you are now in a position to negotiate with your partner. In a spirit of cooperation, explore together where the flexibility is. This is a wonderful opportunity to use humor to lessen any tension that may have arisen between you. It helps to remember the attitude of the "space between": This is not a tug-of-war between two combatants; it is a joint, cooperative, problem-solving task. The focus is on the information in the circle between you.

NEGOTIATION EXERCISE

Find a partner—it could be your child, your parent, a friend, anyone with whom you want to practice communication skills. Teach the three skills that you will be using. And start with a practice round together. I suggest that you begin with an "I" message of appreciation for the other person. For example, "When you..., I felt...." "When you washed the dishes, I felt glad." Or, "When you invited me skating, I felt really happy." Have your partner mirror you and then give you an "I" message of appreciation for you, which you will mirror back.

Now you are ready to negotiate together. For purposes of practice, pick a simple situation to negotiate with each other. It may be choosing a TV program to watch, or what to have for dinner, or where to walk. For starters, practice with situations that are not too loaded. As you become accustomed to using the tools, you can proceed to negotiate a more problematic situation together. Build up to larger issues, those with a greater emotional charge such as where to spend the next major holiday, or how to budget the family's finances, or whether to have a baby.

It may sometimes be useful to provide extra protection to the negotiation process, especially when large issues or feelings are being dealt with or when more than two people are involved. One device is to use a timer to ensure that each person has equal time to talk. Or the speaker can hold a token object—the Native Americans used a feather. The rule is, only the one with the token may speak. The others are listeners. When the one talking has said his or her "peace," the token is passed to whomever wants to speak next. Everyone else is to maintain receptive silence.

Another way to protect the negotiation is to put a boundary around it from the start, agreeing that after a certain prearranged period of time the discussion will end, for now. This could be fifteen minutes or half an hour. In any negotiation, when you can no longer express yourself skillfully or receive information without a great deal of discomfort, take time out. Sometimes there is no available negotiation. Still there is left to you the choice of *how you respond*. That cannot be taken away.

As you practice, remember that the keys to successful negotiation are to keep your focus on the "space between," to remember to use humor, and to add the protection of time limits.

Next, we will consider situations when negotiation fails. The attitude of cooperative problem solving has given way to mounting tension, anger is escalating, and we feel the communication process is getting out of control.

5 The "Silent Scream" and Other Rage Reduction Techniques

Suppose you have been using the communication skills described thus far in a particular situation. In spite of your initial good will and calm beginning, you now feel tight, angry, and you or your partner are sounding more fiery. The discussion is on its way to becoming a raging fight. This section suggests skillful ways to deal with anger gone amuck.

PREVENTING WAR IN THE LIVING ROOM

We have all seen the slogans that pertain to making peace not war: "Arms are for hugging," "Make love not war," "Wage peace." How are we to do this in our personal lives? There are times when we feel the tension building: Like a volcano about to erupt, we feel all out of control.

I believe the most skillful response is to leave, fast. Discharge the rage elsewhere rather than inflicting it on the other person. Rage is a powerful force. It does violence to our emotional bodies and is not unlike a physical explosion to our physical bodies. An out-of-control, enraged person is like a highly charged bundle of explosives.

An analogy illustrates this. If you were to feel a sudden attack of diarrhea coming on, would you continue to stay in the living room and finish your sentence? No, you would get out fast and to the most appropriate place to have the diarrhea attack. It may not seem as obvious, but I believe it is just as essential to get ourselves out fast to an appropriate place to release our sudden rage attack.

As we become more adept we can announce beforehand, "I'm getting really angry; in another minute I may explode!" This warning may help prevent things from boiling over. Every pressure cooker on the market has a safety valve. Our most reliable safety valves have to do with using time and space. When we feel sufficiently cooled down we can return to the person, the situation, the conflict, and talk things over.

I am making a distinction between anger and rage. By anger I mean the vigorous, life-affirming energy where we stand our ground and forcefully declare, "No!", "Stop!" Rage refers to out-of-control, carried-away, extreme anger. Some people, although they are not physically violent, may go berserk with words and commit mayhem verbally, using words like a sledge hammer to pound another person's emotional being to a pulp.

Rage attacks are hard on relationships and ruinous to the sensitive nervous system. If you find yourself the recipient of another person's rage, my advice is: Get up and leave. Let the person rage to the empty room. You can talk things over afterwards.

ANGER

Anger is an assertive, outward thrust of motion—emotion—energy in motion. For some people, anger of any kind is a difficult emotion to receive (let in) or express (let out). Confrontation with an angry adult may seem alarming if not life-threatening. For others, anger as a response may feel safe in the same way that the best defense is a good offense. Some people seem to be most comfortable with anger, and it becomes their way of expressing passion. Furthermore, anger can feel zesty, life-affirming, vital, orgastic. I believe that some people become addicted to anger, that is, their body chemistry has become habituated to a physiological state of the adrenalin excitement of anger, the feeling of "a rush," of being "wired" or aroused.

The obverse side of anger is depression—a vulnerable, soft-belly feeling of being wounded. Psychoanalytic theory has held that depression is anger turned inward, against the self.

Sometimes people who have trouble expressing their anger directly, perhaps due to some inhibition that it is "not nice" or that "civilized people don't," may pair up with those for whom direct expression of anger comes easily. And they may forever after do a two-step with each other, one person subtly goading the other into being twice as angry, expressing anger for them both. To borrow from Alcoholics Anonymous terminology, this may describe the enabler to a rage-aholic.

A final word about anger and what makes us angry— or more accurately, how we allow ourselves to become angry. I believe a large part of our anger comes from the expectation we hold about a certain situation or person: that it won't rain on our beach outing, for example.

Expectations are fine; we can hardly live and plan without them. The culprit is our inability to release from our expectations. Then our attention and our capacity to respond are seriously divided. Our focus on what we *expected* to happen becomes an obstacle to our responding fully to just what *is* happening. As you begin to notice what sets off your anger, see if you have caught your toe and tripped over an expectation.

DISCHARGING ACCUMULATED EMOTION AND TENSION FROM THE BODY

We would not willingly go without bathing our physical bodies on a regular basis, nor without eating and sleeping every day. I believe it is just as essential to cleanse our emotional bodies of the built-up debris of frustrations and tensions that cling to us like a residue of grime and dirt.

In my psychotherapy practice invariably the time

comes when I ask, "What are your personal rage reduction techniques?" These may be any releases that appeal to the person and are compatible with his or her physical health and capability. Examples are some form of vigorous physical exercise that discharges the body and leaves it feeling spent: running, jogging, bicycle riding, brisk walking, team sports activities, or working out at the gym or the spa.

Besides obvious physical releases—which ideally are scheduled on a weekly basis—I encourage clients to have some emergency rage reduction techniques available to bring out quickly. This could be anything that appeals to you. Examples are: tearing a strong cardboard box with your hands, lashing out at a large rock with a thick rope, chopping wood for the fireplace, or scrubbing the kitchen floor. In other words, the anger energy is redirected into physical exercise or useful work.

If nothing satisfies unless it seems really destructive, here are some options using breakables: Go to your local recycling center and smash glass bottles into the receptacles, or pound the aluminum cans flat.

THE "SILENT SCREAM"

One of my favorite personal rage reductions is a technique I call the "silent scream." It can be used at a moment's notice virtually anywhere. All that is required is a small amount of private space such as a bathroom, a walk-in closet, or any separate room.

In a standing position, reach up with your arms as if to draw down air from the sky. Simultaneously take in a large breath through your open mouth. Now tighten up the muscles of the arms and legs, clench the fists, and quickly draw the arms down towards the chest, bending the knees and letting the air out with a loud, but voiceless, breath—"yaagghh"—squeezing all the breath out. Again, straighten the legs and stretch up towards the sky, take in a large breath, and intensely release on the outbreath as before. Just a few repetitions of this cycle will discharge a lot of tension.

These suggestions are a beginning. The rage reduction techniques that will work best for you are the ones you come up with yourself. It is skillful to incorporate rage reduction into your regular routine.

STRESS REDUCTION

Because rage reduction techniques address built-up tension and anger, to be effective I believe they will necessarily be active, vigorous, and physically tiring. But there are many stress releases besides those for anger, some of which are quite passive and soothing.

I like to consider the options for stress release in terms of the four elements as defined by the ancients: air, earth, water, and fire. Freely given, they are our earthly heritage, widely available for our use. They are perfectly natural, non-drug, therapeutic agents that we can use for our healing. They may be used in any combination with our four bodies: the physical, the emotional, the mental, and the spiritual. Here are some examples.

Air

We use the air continuously in our breathing. To use it as a stress release, find a place where the air is freshest. With focused attention, inhale and exhale with the attitude that you are calming the mind. Experiment with the depth and rhythm of your breathing: slower, faster, find what feels good to you. Regular, deliberate breathing has a quieting effect on the mind. Another way to use the air for stress release is by walking outdoors, or jogging, running, bicycling, etc.

Earth

For relieving anxiety and a certain spacey, ungrounded feeling, the earth is the best choice. Some ways to use the earth for grounding are to plunge your hands and feet into the soil, or to engage in any form of gardening. It is also grounding and stabilizing to eat certain cooked vegetables: roots such as potatoes, beets, or carrots. Another way to use the earth for steadying your emotions is to work with potters clay or with bread dough.

Walking in nature, among trees or in a garden or a field, can energize us when we are low. A favorite rejuvenation exercise of mine involves the use of a tree. Choose a robust tree that you can sit right up against, gently pressing your head and spine into the tree trunk. Close your eyes and in a receptive attitude breath in the tree's vital energy, feel its vigor recharging you. As you breath, be aware of the cooperative exchange of oxygen and carbon dioxide going on between you and the tree. Can you sense the flow of sap behind the tree bark? At the end of your stay, you may want to thank the tree.

Water

A frequent use of water for releasing tension is a long soak in a full tub of hot water. While it is soothing to the physical body, I think of it as benefiting primarily the emotional body. Accumulated pain and tension are drawn out into the warm water and then down the drain and into the earth, which accepts and absorbs it.

Another way to use water as an emotional cleanser is to drink it, plenty of it, daily. And while drinking, have the attitude that you are cleansing the inside of your body, as indeed you are. Sitting or walking by a stream, a river, a lake, or the ocean can also feel healing.

Fire

The chief representative of fire is the sun. While care must be taken to protect the skin, due to the depletion of the ozone layer, the sun is still a powerful healer bringing warmth, light, and vitality. Explore ways in which you can safely use the sun for converting negative stress energy into a sense of positive well-being.

Burning what you have written—seeing it cleanly consumed by fire—can be a powerful stress release. (Fire purifies and reveals the pure gold from the dross with which it was mixed.) Or just watching a campfire can feel healing. Another, quieting use of fire is to light a candle and relax in its soft glow.

FORGIVENESS AND HOW TO SAY "I'M SORRY"

We may struggle inwardly between our anger and our deep desire to forgive. Staying honest with ourselves is important. We can be patient, extending to ourselves the same courtesy that we would give to another. Sooner or later it is in our own best interest, for our own growth, to begin the practice of forgiveness. We can be kindly bent towards ourselves as we learn this and other life lessons.

How to say "I'm sorry": Speak the truth and be sincere. First we negotiate with ourselves: Given this person or this situation, what do I choose to do or to say. We may want to ask the other person how we can say "I'm sorry" in a way that feels so to him or her, asking, "Is there anything I can say or do that will show you I am sorry?" Or, "How can I tell you, how can I show you, that I'm sorry?"

In the preceeding pages, techniques for skillful communication have been presented. They can be easily learned and, once learned, improved with practice. Now we have reached the end of techniques and approach the core of the matter, where communication becomes art. I call it, listening with the heart.

6 *Listening with the Heart*

There is a hunger, a yearning to feel valued and loved by the other. More than declarations of love, or gifts of jewels or chocolates, that which satisfies this hunger is the feeling of being received and accepted. The technique of mirroring gives a taste of this. The full development requires from us more...

WHEN COMMUNICATION BECOMES COMMUNING

Listening with the heart is an open-hearted attitude that conveys a feeling of peace, patience, and receptiveness. It is an inclining towards the other that connotes there is time, I have time for you. It is a willingness to be available to you in a simple act of listening, knowing that in doing so I am not giving up my autonomy as a separate individual. Simply for now I voluntarily set aside my preferences and points of view, and receive you with patience, without judgement. Listening with the heart is a mood we create by our willingness to let in another person's expressions, thoughts, and feelings. When we listen with our hearts we become open, available, and accessible to the other. This brings us close and creates a feeling of intimacy. It is a gift of love, a gift of ourselves, of our time and our attentiveness.

THE USE OF SILENCE

We will find when we are listening with the heart that we use silence—plenty of it! We make eye contact when possible. And we give occasional brief comments—"umhmm" will do—just to convey that we are listening. Perhaps we ask an open-ended question from time to time to invite more communication. But even this is not necessary when your partner feels that you are listening with your heart.

LISTENING EXERCISE

When teaching communication skills in group trainings, I invariably have included the following exercise to emphasize the use of silence as a skill. This exercise will require about an hour.

Find a partner with whom to take turns listening. Sit facing each other. Decide which one will listen for the first twenty minutes. The one whose turn it is to talk may choose any situation or relationship, but the exercise will be more meaningful if the issue has emotional value for the speaker.

The one who is listening should keep an alert, attentive body posture and maintain eye contact with the speaker, whether or not it is reciprocated. Try to avoid editorial comments such as shaking the head or saying, "I know just how you feel," etc. Be still, and listen.

When it is your turn to listen, you may notice a tendency to start to interject comments. You may observe your mind chattering with all the thoughts and comments it wants to say, remarks that would detract from the speaker such as, "That reminds me of the time when I...." Don't.

Perhaps you notice also the tendency to begin to give helpful advice or to solve the problem. Listening with the heart is not concerned with these. Often problem solving and advice giving are devices to relieve us of our own discomfort, to give us the feeling that we are doing something. Practice being still; just listen.

At the end of twenty minutes, finish what is being said and then switch roles. Do not at this time comment on your experience of the process. There will be time for that at the end. Let the person whose turn to speak comes next, talk about something entirely separate from what has gone before. This is not a time for building on the first speaker's issue or for making any comments on what has already been said.

At the end of twenty minutes, let the one who has been talking stop. So far this exercise has taken forty minutes. For the remaining twenty minutes, take turns telling each other what the process was like, both as the one listening and as the one speaking. Please note that this exchange is not about commenting on the *content* of what either one has said, only on the *experience of the exercise*. In feedback at group trainings, it is poignant how often people discover that never before have they had the experience of really being listened to.

When we listen with the heart, we listen intently with our whole being and allow ourselves to take in not only the information or content of the other person's communication but also his or her feelings. What a person expresses is also a good key to what he or she may be experiencing. Someone who dwells on critical comments about other persons or situations is saying, in effect, "Things aren't right with me." Someone who dwells on recounting accidents and injuries may be expressing his or her anxiety, even though the accident happened to another. A person who focuses on stories having to do with pain and loss may be expressing feelings of depression. We are always—no matter what we are saying or whom we believe we are telling about—only expressing ourselves. We can hardly do otherwise. As we practice listening with the heart we will become more attuned to the whole being of the other person. Much more will be revealed to us as we become receptive.

We need to teach others how we want to be listened to. They cannot read our minds. Others depend on us to tell them what we want them to know. It is also important that we acknowledge their attempts to listen in the way we want to be received, by expressing our appreciation for any positive efforts we perceive in that direction.

Listening with the heart is the central core where communication becomes communing. By our open attentiveness we convey our willingness to receive the other person's thoughts and feelings, drawing close in a shared communion. Listening is an art. Sometimes, more often than not, all that is required is that we listen with the heart.

Afterword

In the Introduction, I alluded to the four main aspects of a person that can be likened to bodies: the physical, the mental, the emotional, and the spiritual. Here is a further elaboration of this model for understanding ourselves. Of course a model is merely a way to look at a whole structure. But let us see what may be learned by considering these aspects of ourselves separately.

The Physical

By the physical body I am referring to the concrete, tangible, material form of a person. The physical body undergoes extraordinary change and growth throughout a lifetime, beginning at infancy on into childhood, through puberty to full adulthood, and ending in old age. This the body does without any need for deliberate effort or conscious control on the part of an individual. Indeed, under usual circumstances it seems that the process is automatic and cannot be stopped. From toothless beginnings as babes, over the course of time teeth grow in—two sets—and given long enough, may decay and fall out.

If a person wishes to develop certain skill with the body, a concerted, deliberate effort must be made. To become an Olympic swimmer, a tennis pro, or an expert gymnast one perseveres in training the physical body for mastery in these specific areas. However, given sufficient maintenance the physical body grows, seemingly of its own accord.

The Mental

The growth of the mental aspect of a person parallels in some ways that of the physical body, that is, certain maturational stages for mental, or cognitive, growth—especially in the area of problem-solving capabilities—seem to correlate with the individual's physical growth and development.

However, a major part of mental development is not at all automatic. It takes determination to acquire verbal language skills, even more to learn the alphabet and to become fully literate. Mastery of even the rudiments of formal education, the " 3 R's," hardly occurs automatically. To achieve expertise in a chosen intellectual discipline requires great strength of will and focused effort, just as to attain physical proficiency. We are fortunate to live in a culture that places great value on mental development. Through the public education system a motivated student can continue to develop mentally from the lower grades all the way to the university level, and attain an advanced degree in his or her chosen field.

The Emotional

The emotional body refers to our feeling nature and is the basis of our capacity for close relationships with others. Psychologists believe that this aspect of ourselves, too, follows a developmental sequence. Beginning at birth with deep bonding to the mothering figure, an individual's emotional growth continues in an ever outward-reaching network of relationships which involve the father, siblings, grandparents, playmates, teachers, neighbors and others, and at puberty focuses on peer relationships. This developmental sequence reaches maturity in an adult in a love relationship with an intimate other. From the culmination of that union the entire cycle may repeat, throughout generations.

Our emotional growth is rather hit and miss, and depends on the emotional wisdom of our parents and early first caregivers. Deliberate, intentional skill building in this area has been largely overlooked. Where do we go to acquire proficiency in developing the emotional aspects of ourselves, skills in emotional self-expression and relationships?

Recently opportunities to acquire tools for emotional growth have become more accessible in our culture. Various psychotherapies and counseling techniques for individuals as well as for couples and families, workshops and classes, AA and related peer support groups are widely available. Some public schools offer elective courses in peer counseling, and classes in parenting skills are provided by some community agencies and PTAs. It seems that we are at the beginning of a movement that is gaining momentum, to focus attention on the development of proficiencies in the emotional and relational realms of our beings.

The Spiritual

This brings us to that most hidden of all aspects of ourselves, the spiritual body. "Subtler than the subtlest," our awareness of this body may come, or not, in a lifetime. By spiritual I mean the relationship of the "little" self, or the personality encased in the body, with the "larger" self, the transpersonal or transcendent perspective wherein the individual powerfully experiences himself or herself to be part of the larger whole.

Many people seem to live their lives without coming into conscious awareness of the spiritual part of themselves. But as with the other aspects of our beings, its deliberate or intentional development seems to be greatly assisted by a teacher or teachings, as well as by certain exercises and disciplines such as physical and mental purification and techniques of concentration like meditation. The ultimate development of the spiritual aspect is said to be exemplified by the mystic who is self-realized, that is, one who has transcended the ordinary waking consciousness of the personal self and, having overcome the feeling of separation of the personal self, identifies in a profound way with the whole of life.

COMMUNICATION SKILLS TRAINING
IN PUBLIC SCHOOLS

I would like training in communication skills to be offered to large numbers of young people. Our schools already attend to the physical and mental development of school children, by offering programs that include physical education as well as academic subjects. I would like to see the curriculum expanded to include the emotional development of students as well, by teaching specific relationship skills such as the communication skills presented here.

Already programs exist in assertiveness training and conflict resolution, some of them geared for the classroom and others that could easily be adapted. These trainings usually have been offered to public schools as an optional enrichment program on a contractual basis, if offered at all. I would like to see these and similar techniques for skillful communication and relationships become a regular part of public school education, thereby reaching large numbers of the next generation of humanity.

COMMUNICATION SKILLS
AND HEALING THE EARTH

There are larger ramifications to learning and practicing communication skills. The first obvious advantage is to ourselves. It simply feels better to get along harmoniously with the people in our lives. With practice we can become more confident of our communication skills, more aware and respectful of our own and other people's boundaries, and more at ease in negotiating with ourselves and with others.

As we carry a spirit of friendship and cooperation into our households, our neighborhoods, and our places of work, then we may begin to look for the expansion of this peace extending out from us in all directions and over the whole planet. I believe there is a true teaching in the lines of the well-known peace song, "Let there be peace on earth, and let it begin with me."

I have never heard anyone say that he or she did not want peace. We all claim to want world peace. But how do we expect peace between nations until we have peace in our homes. Nations are, after all, collections of people.

I believe that we are, each one of us, participants in a vast drama of evolution, that the future of humanity depends on you and me, and on all the other you's and me's who now occupy the planet. We have arrived at this place in our collective understanding by the energies of all those who have gone before. I believe that there are far-reaching opportunities and consequences set in motion by the decisions we make in our living rooms and in our day to day interactions, that all our expressions and actions are consequential, and that you and I are part of the leaven on which humanity depends to rise. Seen from this perspective, wouldn't you— in your own life— want to give the evolution of humanity all you've got?

Suggested Reading

These are some books that I have found particularly helpful:

Faber, Adele and Mazlish, Elaine. *How to Talk So Kids Will Listen and Listen So Kids Will Talk*. New York: Avon, 1980.

Ginott, Haim. *Between Parent and Child*. New York: Macmillan, 1965.

Keyes, Ken, Jr. *Handbook to Higher Consciousness*. Coos Bay, OR: Love Line Books, 1975.

Pilgrim, Peace. *Peace Pilgrim: Her Life and Work in Her Own Words*. Santa Fe: Ocean Tree Books, 1982.